GETTING OLD
IS A JOKE

GETTING OLD IS A JOKE

Edited by

JUDY BROWN

Ronnie Sellers Productions, Inc.

ACKNOWLEDGMENTS

◆

First: I'd like to thank all the comedians whose memento morte gags remind us to laugh through the second half of our lives.

Second: I'd like to thank Robin Haywood and the merry pranksters at Ronnie Sellers Productions, Inc., for looking into the future and choosing to giggle at it. Hey everybody, have fun tonight.

—Judy Brown

Published by Ronnie Sellers Productions, Inc.

Edited by Ari Meil

Publishing Director: Robin Haywood
Managing Editor: Mary Baldwin
Editorial Assistant: Lizzie Stewart
Assistant Production Editor: Kathy Fisher
Designer: George Corsillo, Design Monsters

81 West Commerical Street, Portland, Maine 04101
For ordering information:
Phone: 1-800-MAKE-FUN (800-625-3386)
Fax: (207) 772-6814
Visit our Web site: www.rsvp.com
E-mail: rsp@rsvp.com

ISBN 10: 1-56906-972-7
ISBN 13: 978-1-56906-972-1

Printed and bound in India.

FOREWORD

◆

Getting old is a joke. At least I fervently hope so, because I'm getting older by the moment and could use a laugh. If you are also aging every minute of the day, every day of the week, and every week of every year, I prescribe these nearly 150 laughs, giggles, chuckles, and guffaws. (Phew, I'm not as young as I used to be, and I now need to take a breather even after writing a long sentence.) Laughter is the best medicine, and what with the Medicare D plan, it may be the only one us agesters will be able to afford.

Have fun,
Judy
judybrowni@usa.net
www.judybrown.info

SECTION

The Truth Is . . . You're Old!

Old age isn't so bad when you consider
the alternative.

—MAURICE CHEVALIER

You know you're getting
older when the candles
cost more than the cake.

–BOB HOPE

◆

"Don't worry about senility," my
grandfather used to say. "When
it hits you, you won't know it."

–BILL COSBY

Old people reach an age when they decide not to look when they back out of the driveway. They just think, "Well, I'm old, and I'm backing up. I survived; let's see if you can."

—JERRY SEINFELD

I was able to find my original birth certificate, but it took three guys to help me get it. Stone tablets are heavy.

—BOB HOPE

You know you're getting old when you find yourself in the mall saying, "A cane that's also a chair? Wow!"

—RENO GOODALE

There are certain signs that you're getting old. I walked past a cemetery, and two guys ran after me with shovels.

—RODNEY DANGERFIELD

When you get older your body changes. I've noticed it myself. Now I groan louder after meals than I do after an orgasm.

—JOEL WARSHAW

You know you're getting old when
you stoop to tie your shoelaces and
wonder what else you could do while
you're down there.

—GEORGE BURNS

My aunt lost her glasses.
She spent 20 minutes
nagging a coat rack.

—HENNY YOUNGMAN

◆

You know you're getting
older when it takes you
more time to recover than
it did to tire you out.

—MILTON BERLE

They say that you
learn something new
every day. But I'm at
the age where I unlearn
something new every day.

—JANICE HEISS

You know you're not a
kid anymore when you're
obsessed with the thermostat.

—JEFF FOXWORTHY

When I was a boy, the
Dead Sea was only sick.

—GEORGE BURNS

You know you're old when they've
discontinued your blood type.

–PHYLLIS DILLER

Old is when your doctor
no longer X-rays you. He
just holds you up to the light.

–RED BUTTONS

You know you've reached middle age when you're cautioned to slow down by your doctor, instead of by the police.

—JOAN RIVERS

When I was younger, I used to
have a photographic memory.
Now it takes three hours to develop.

— JERRY RUBIN

I'm officially middle-aged, and I don't
need drugs anymore, thank God.
I can get the same effect just by
standing up real fast.

— JONATHAN KATZ

I'm not really wrinkled.
I just had a nap on a
chenille bedspread.

—PHYLLIS DILLER

You know you're not a kid
anymore when you point out
what buildings used to be where.

—JEFF FOXWORTHY

You know you're getting old
when work is a lot less fun —
and fun is a lot more work.

—JOAN RIVERS

I'm now old enough to
personally identify every
object in antiques stores.

—ANITA MILNER

I'm at an age where my back
goes out more than I do.

—PHYLLIS DILLER

My parents retired to an
island in Florida full of
old people who do whatever
they want all day. It's like
Lord of the Flies with walkers.

—PENELOPE LOMBARD

You know you're 50 when
the "good" side of the bed
is next to the bathroom
and the humidifier.

—RICHARD SMITH

First you forget names,
then you forget faces.
Next you forget to pull
your zipper up and finally,
you forget to pull it down.

—GEORGE BURNS

You know you're old when
your walker has an airbag.

–PHYLLIS DILLER

I can tell I'm getting older,
because I find myself using
words like "spacious," "roomy,"
and "comfortable" when I'm
buying underwear.

–RENO GOODALE

◆

I've been around the block so many times, sidewalks crack when they see me coming.

—KATHERINE GRIFFITH

I've been around the block so many

You know you're old when obscene phone calls make you chuckle.

—RICHARD SMITH

SECTION

At Least You've Got Your Health

I recently had my annual physical examination, which I get once every seven years, and when the nurse weighed me, I was shocked to discover how much stronger the Earth's gravitational pull has become.

—DAVE BARRY

It's great to have gray hair.
Ask anyone who's bald.

—RODNEY DANGERFIELD

It's no longer a question of
staying healthy. It's a question
of finding a sickness you like.

—JACKIE MASON

You know you're getting old
when all the names in your
black book have MD after them.

—ARNOLD PALMER

I don't plan to grow
old gracefully. I plan
to have facelifts until
my ears meet.

—RITA RUDNER

They say aging is a funny thing,
but there's nothing funny about it.
You still feel 14, but when you turn
on the bathroom light, this ugly old
guy in the mirror leaps out at you.

—ERIC IDLE

A man brags about his new
hearing aid: "It's the most
expensive one I've ever had.
It cost $2,500." His friend asks,
"What kind is it?" And the man
says, "Half-past four."

—HENNY YOUNGMAN

When your friends begin
to flatter you on how young
you look, it's a sure sign
you're getting old.

–MARK TWAIN

◆

For those of us getting
up in years, weightlifting
consists of standing up.

–MILTON BERLE

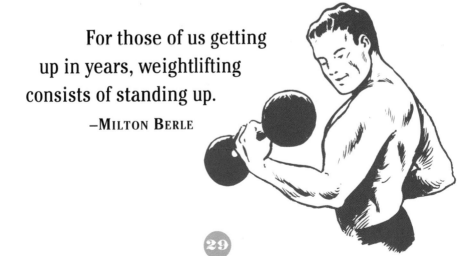

I know I'm getting older, because
I pulled my shoulder out putting
peanut butter on a bagel. At least
it was chunky, though.

—JEFF CESARIO

◆

After 40, every day is Halloween: you
wake up with a different face than the
one you went to sleep with, and it
ain't pretty. And the "I just
woke up" face of your 40s
is the "all-day face" of
your 50s.

—MEG MALY

If you don't wear your glasses
when you look in the mirror,
you can't see your wrinkles.

—MILTON BERLE

I'm getting older and I'm thinking
about having my eggs frozen. Well,
just the egg whites. I'm trying to cut
back on my cholesterol.

—BRENDA PONTIFF

31

I'm at an age where I should get in shape, but it's probably not going to happen. Quite frankly, I'm so lazy, I'd drive to my bathroom, if I could.

—MICHELE BALAN

The older you get, the higher you wear your underwear. It's just like rings on a tree. By the time you're 80, 90 years old, your breasts are inside them. When you die, they just pull them up over your head.

—MARGARET SMITH

I don't know how you feel about old age, but in my case I didn't even see it coming. It hit me from the rear.

—PHYLLIS DILLER

Bald men. They get older and gravity starts sucking their hair back into their scalp, and shooting it out their ears.

—MARYELLEN HOOPER

Just think: we're the first
society to kill off our old
people with childproof caps.

—STRANGE DE JIM

I'm at that age where
everything is starting
to click — my knees,
my elbows, my neck . . .

—MILTON BERLE

My dad's pants kept creeping up on him. By 65 he was just a pair of pants and a head.

—JEFF ALTMAN

You know you're getting old when you're more attractive hanging upside down.

—CATHY LADMAN

You're not a kid anymore
when you've owned clothes
so long that they've come
back into style … twice.

—JEFF FOXWORTHY

When I wake up in the morning,
it takes me a half hour to find
my glasses, just so I can look
for my teeth, so I can tell my
wife to find my hair.

—RICHARD JENI

People used to tell me I had great hair. Then I lost it, and now they say I have a great smile. I'm getting kind of nervous.

—Don McLysaght

A doctor said to his patient, "You're going to live until you're 80." The patient said, "I am 80." The doctor replied, "What did I tell you?"

—Henny Youngman

I'm at the "Ma'am" stage of life. But you shouldn't be called "Ma'am" until you've had that first mammogram.

—MARGARET SMITH

It's true that gray hair makes you look distinguished. It distinguishes you from the younger-looking people.

—KELLY

I have trouble adjusting to new bifocals.
I have to keep looking up and down to
get things in focus. My grandson calls
me Grandma Bobblehead.

—Charlotte Lobb

My sister Kathryn has some crazy ideas
about getting older. After 40 years as a
brunette, when her hair turned white
she decided that she'd become an albino.
Yeah, Sis, and your wrinkles mean you're
a shar-pei.

—Darly Hogue

SECTION

3

Till Death Do Us Part

Doctors say an active sex life can help a person lead a healthier and longer life. Here's my question: Where do you go to get that prescription filled?

—JAY LENO

Don't talk to me about Valentine's Day. At my age an affair of the heart is a bypass.

—JOAN RIVERS

An 80-year-old man is planning to marry a 20-year-old woman, and his friend warns, "This marriage could be fatal." The old man answers, "If she dies, she dies."

—MILTON BERLE

I'm at the age where food has taken the place of sex in my life. In fact, I've just had a mirror put over my kitchen table.

—RODNEY DANGERFIELD

———————————◆———————————

You know you're not a kid anymore when you can live without sex, but not without your glasses.

—JEFF FOXWORTHY

The best contraceptive for old people is nudity.

—PHYLLIS DILLER

I was talking to this cute young woman who said she had a thing for older men. I got all excited and asked, "What is it?" She said, "Pepper spray."

—CHUCK JOHNSON

Statistics show that the older you are when you get married, the more likely it is you'll stay together. Of course, because at 85 you can't hear how boring he is.

—CHRISTINE O'ROURKE

Sex at an advanced age is like trying to shoot pool with a rope.

—GEORGE BURNS

I've always dated older men.
But it's gotten to the point that
if I want to date someone older
than me, I'll have to go to the
cemetery and dig him up.

—TONYA MOON

In a survey for *Modern Maturity*
magazine, men over 75 said they
had sex once a week. Which proves
that old guys lie about sex, too.

—IRV GILMAN

I'm getting old. When I squeeze
into a tight parking space, I'm
sexually satisfied for the day.

—RODNEY DANGERFIELD

Making love used to make
my toes curl, now it just
gives me foot cramps.

—KATHIE DICE

I didn't realize I was getting old until my attorney advised me to get my affairs in order. Okay, so now I have Andy on Monday, Bob on Tuesday, and the FedEx man on Wednesday.

—KATHERINE POEHLMANN

I know I'm getting old because I carry Tums in my pocket. I used to carry condoms, but now I know it's more likely that I'll get a stomachache than I'll get laid.

—JOHN HEFFRON

Some people say older men have long endurance and can make love longer. Let's think about this: Who wants to have sex with an old man for a long time?

—MARSHA WARFIELD

They say men get sexier as they get older. No, sexy men get sexier as they get older, the rest of us get red sports cars.

—JEFF SHAW

There are things I could do when I was younger that I can't do anymore. Like have a conversation with my wife without getting yelled at.

—RENO GOODALE

An 80-year-old woman in Pakistan is pregnant. You know what she said? "Damn prom."

—CRAIG KILBORN

My grandmother's 90 and she's dating. He's 93. They're very happy, they never argue. Of course, they can't hear each other.

—Cathy Ladman

My mother on *The Dating Game*, how great would that be? "Bachelor Number Two: We're at a dinner dance at the temple, I fall and break a hip, do you: A. Stay with me on the dance floor, B. Run and get help, C. Leave me there to *drop dead just like my kids would.*"

—Judy Gold

Here's To You, Gramps

My grandfather started walking five miles a day when he was 82. He's 90 now, and we don't know where the hell he is.

—Ellen DeGeneres

My grandmother was a very
tough woman. She buried
three husbands. Two of
them were just napping.

–RITA RUDNER

I was watching the Superbowl with my
92-year-old grandfather. His team
scored a touchdown. When they showed
the instant replay, he thought they
scored another one. I was gonna tell
him, but I figured the game he was
watching was better.

–STEVEN WRIGHT

◆

With my kid I don't get no respect.
I told him, "You're young, you don't
have it upstairs." He said, "You're
old, you don't have it downstairs."

–RODNEY DANGERFIELD

My grandmother is 85 years old,
and she's starting to lose her
memory. Everybody's upset about
it except me, because she sent me
eight checks for my birthday this
year. Hey, that's 40 bucks.

–TOM ARNOLD

I just saw my grandmother,
probably for the last time.
She's not sick or anything,
she just bores the hell out of me.

—A. WHITNEY BROWN

I'm kinda depressed right now,
because we had to put my
grandfather in a rest home.
Well, not actually, we didn't
have the money. So we drove
down the turnpike, and put
him in a rest area.

—RICH VOS

Today I picked up Grandma Kilby at the airport. She's at that age where she doesn't remember things well. So I said, "Thanks for coming, goodbye!"

—CRAIG KILBORN

My nana is 90 years old and she's still driving. Not with me, of course. I'm not that stupid.

—TIM ALLEN

Even when my mother was 88
years old, she never used glasses.
She drank right out of the bottle!

—HENNY YOUNGMAN

My grandfather lived to be 103 years old,
and every morning he would eat an entire
raw onion and smoke a cigar. You know
what his dying words were? Nobody does.
They couldn't get near the guy.

—JONATHAN KATZ

I remember my own dear grandfather. He smoked and drank every day of his life until he was 81. Then we had to kill him.

—ROSEANNE BARR

My grandfather is a little forgetful, and he likes to give me advice. One day he took me aside, and left me there.

—RON RICHARDS

When I die, I want to go peacefully
like my grandfather did, in his sleep.
Not screaming, like the passengers
in his car.

—MICHAEL JEFFREYS

I've been storing my grandmother
in Florida, but now I want to move
her north to cooler weather.
I figure she'll keep better.

—LARRY AMOROS

God bless my mom, she had reverse Alzheimers. Towards the end she remembered everything, and she was pissed.

—S. RACHEL LOVEY

Ronald Reagan was 77 years old at the end of his presidency, and he had access to the button. The button! My grandfather is 77, and we won't let him use the remote control to the TV set.

—DENNIS MILLER

I will never forget the day my grandmother died, mostly because I won the pool.

—BRENT CUSHMAN

I've got an uncle who's 92, and people that age, their whole social life revolves around going to funerals. And why not? The funeral home is a great place to go when you're 92: There's free parking, it's well lit, somebody opens the door, there's free coffee downstairs. And there's always somebody a little worse off than you.

—JOHN DAVID SIDLEY

My husband's granny is 87, and she just got two new hearing aides, and cataracts removed from both eyes. I tell her we're going to fix her up just a little more and then sell her.

—TINA FEY

I'll always remember my grandfather's last words: "A truck!"

—EMO PHILIPS

My dad is 86 years old and he's still working, God bless him. He's a pimp, and he's out there every night.

—JONATHAN KATZ

My father refuses to wear his hearing aid. But that's okay, because, as he says, "People don't mind repeating themselves three times." Yeah sure, Dad. Forget your glasses, too, and you won't see them give you the finger.

—JUDY BROWN

My grandmother lives in Florida now. She just moved . . . which is great because we thought that coma was permanent.

—MYQ KAPLAN

◆

I only have one grandpa. We call him Grandpa Alive. He still beats me at checkers, but I kick his ass at full-contact karate.

—DAVE ATTELL

SECTION

Older Is Wiser

What I look forward to is continued immaturity followed by death.

—DAVE BARRY

My parents moved to Florida. They didn't want to, but they're in their 60s, and that's the law. The leisure police pull up in front of the old peoples' home in a golf cart and say, "Let's go, Pop. White belt, white pants, white shoes: Get in the back."

—JERRY SEINFELD

You can live to be a hundred if you give up all the things that make you want to live to be a hundred.

—WOODY ALLEN

There's a simple secret for
long life: Get to be a hundred,
and then be careful!

—MILTON BERLE

The oldest bank robber in the United States, a
92-year-old man in Texas, has been sentenced
to 12 years in prison. This is what scares
me about our prison system. You know
with good behavior he could be out
and back on the streets by the
time he's 98.

—JAY LENO

There's one advantage to being 102. No peer pressure.
—DENNIS WOLFBERG

The other day at an Australian track meet, a 101-year-old man ran a mile and set a world record for people over 100 years old. There is some controversy concerning the record though, because when the man began the race he was only 98.
—CONAN O'BRIEN

❖

When you're young you say, "If I become a vegetable, pull the plug!" When you get older you hedge a little. "If I'm a turnip, kill me. If I'm a trendier vegetable, like radicchio, mist me twice a day and trim the wilted leaves."

—DANIEL LIEBERT

◆

My uncle lives in an assisted living home near a college campus, and I've discovered something: These assisted living homes are college dorms for old people. They play the music too loud, and they complain about the same stuff. "I don't like the food. I don't have enough money. Where are my drugs?"

—JOHN DAVID SIDLEY

The nicest thing about being in my 60s is that I know I'm not going to die in my 50s.

—BILL WIGGINS

According to the oldest person in the world, a 121-year-old French woman, the secret to long life is to start every day with a little bit of olive oil. That's not new, Popeye's been doing that for years.

—JAY LENO

A 98-year-old man has graduated from college. My advice to the guy is to take a few years off, go travel, and get your head together.

—CRAIG KILBORN

A 90-year-old Florida man won a $16,000,000 lottery. He's using the money to start a foundation to help him remember where he left his pants.

—CONAN O'BRIEN

America's oldest person has died at 113. Police are questioning her fiercely competitive 112-year-old roommate.

—CONAN O'BRIEN

I used to camp out for tickets to rock concerts. Now you could tell me that Barbra Streisand is playing for free down the street, and I'd say, "How far down the street? Let's just stay here and watch the Discovery Channel. C'mon, it's Shark Week!"

—KATHLEEN MADIGAN

In Connecticut, Glastonbury High awarded Thomas Hennessy his high school diploma at the age of 102. Way to go, Thomas. In today's world, without a diploma, you've got no future.

—NORM MACDONALD

By the time you're 80 years old you've learned everything. You only have to remember it.

—GEORGE BURNS

If you live to be 100, you've got it made.
Very few people die past that age.

—GEORGE BURNS

Here's some sad news: The world's oldest
man has died in Japan at the age of a hundred
and fourteen. What's the deal with this "world's
oldest" title? It's like some kind of curse, have
you noticed? As soon as you get it, like a year
later, you're dead.

—JAY LENO

An 86-year-old man started driving around the world today. He backed out of the driveway and ran into his mailbox.

—CRAIG KILBORN

Oklahoma State University's oldest graduate, 62-year-old Steven Baker Little, formerly alcoholic and homeless, earned a degree in English. Ironically, in today's job market, an English degree best qualifies a person to become an alcoholic homeless man.

—JIMMY FALLON

SECTION

Getting Old Is A Joke

Looking 50 is great, if you're 60.

–JOAN RIVERS

At 88, how do you feel when getting up in the morning? Amazed.

−GEORGE BURNS

◆

The oldest man in the world passed away yesterday at the age of 112. The cause of death, say doctors, was being 112.

−CONAN O'BRIEN

The secret of staying
young is to live honestly, eat
slowly, and lie about your age.

—LUCILLE BALL

◆

Middle age is that time
of life when you can
afford to lose a golf ball,
but you can't hit it that far.

—MILTON BERLE

Middle age is when your age starts to show around your middle.

—BOB HOPE

I'm pushing 40. At least, I think that's how much I can bench.

—JEFF SHAW

My sex life is nothing to
crow about. At my age
I'm envious of a stiff wind.

—RODNEY DANGERFIELD

The Pillsbury Doughboy
is 42 years old. He's at that
age where he goes to the
doctor for an exam and gets
poked on the other side.

—JAY LENO

Age is a question of mind
over matter. If you don't
mind, it doesn't matter.

–JACK BENNY

◆

Just remember, once you're over the
hill you begin to pick up speed.

–CHARLES M. SCHULTZ

No one in my family ages
well. I think somebody
peed in our gene pool.

—RICK SCOTTI

I've heard losing your memory
is a sign of old age. I just can't
remember where I heard it.

—BOB MAIER

I'm so old that when I order
a three-minute egg they
make me pay up front.

—HENNY YOUNGMAN

True terror is to wake up one
morning and discover that your
high school class is running
the country.

—KURT VONNEGUT

You know you're 50 when you read the obituaries not to see who died, but to see how long they lived.

–RICHARD SMITH

You know you're old when your birth certificate was a scroll.

–PHYLLIS DILLER

My husband is 15 years older than I.
He likes to say, "Age is just a number."
Why is it only old people say that?

—TERRI RYBURN-LAMONTE

Don't go to a school reunion. There'll be a lot of old people there claiming to be your classmates.

—TOM DREESEN

A recent study found that during a seven-hour sleep period, a healthy senior will wake 153 times. I bet 152 of those are just to check if he's still alive.

—JOAN RIVERS

One trouble with growing older is that it gets progressively tougher to find a famous historical figure who didn't amount to much when he was your age.

—BILL VAUGHAN

Aging isn't all that bad.
Think of the trouble we'd
be in if wrinkles hurt!

—MILTON BERLE

Many bad things happen when you turn 50.
You can't see, you can't hear, you can read
the entire Oxford English Dictionary in the
time it takes you to go to the bathroom,
and you keep meeting people your own age
who look like Grandpa Walton. And those are
the women.

—DAVE BARRY

Middle age is the time of life
when the most fun you have
is talking about the most fun
you used to have.

—GENE PERRET

◆

I have everything I had
20 years ago, only it's
all a little bit lower.

—GYPSY ROSE LEE

Getting old is a fascinating thing. The older you get, the older you want to get.

—KEITH RICHARDS

◆

The good thing about going to your 25-year high school reunion is that you get to see all your old classmates. The bad thing is that they get to see you.

—ANITA MILNER

Old is always 15
years from now.

        –BILL COSBY

The older I get, the more I
believe we should respect
the elderly.

    –JASON LOVE

The older I get, the simpler the definition of maturity seems: It's the length of time between when I realize someone is a jackass and when I tell them that they are one.

—BRETT BUTLER

A new study shows that estrogen appears to help protect women's memories from decline due to aging. After being given estrogen, researchers found that women once again were able to bring up things their husbands did years ago and throw it back in their faces.

—JOHNNY ROBISH

Is it just me or is there a direct
correlation between the older we get,
and the number of checkers games
that end in draw?

—GREG MANUEL

---◆---

Middle age is when you don't
need a roomful of antiques
to sit down on something
50 years old.

—MILTON BERLE